C000197696

MEET YOUR BRAIN

Contents

Written by Kathryn Kendall Boucher

Collins

1 Meet your brain!

Your brain is one of the largest and most complex organs in your body. Everything you do is controlled by your brain. Your brain is also where your emotions are made.

This brain scan shows the parts of the brain that are activated when we feel pain and empathy.

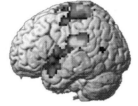 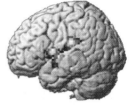

pain   empathy

Evolution of the human brain

It took millions of years for the human brain to become as complex as it is now. Early humans had smaller brains. As humans **evolved**, their brains got bigger and they became more intelligent.

We know human brains have got bigger because human skulls are bigger!

Humans learnt to create fire around 400,000 years ago. Incredibly, this had an important impact on brain development. Humans used fire to cook food, which made it easier to digest. This meant their bodies didn't have to use so much energy digesting meals. The extra energy helped their brains to grow.

Have you ever wondered ...

... why other mammals can walk as soon as they're born but humans can't? It's because of our brains! Animals are born with big, developed brains, but humans are born with small, undeveloped brains. We can't control our bodies until our brains have had time to grow.

Fight or flight

Early humans were hunter-gatherers, which means they roamed around hunting animals and finding plants to eat. It was very dangerous because they could be attacked and killed by wild animals, or even other humans.

Their brains evolved to help them survive. If danger appeared, their brains would act quickly to release hormones that made their bodies ready to either fight the danger or run away as fast as possible. This is called the "fight or flight" response.

The physical signs of the body in fight or flight response are …

dilated pupils: pupils get bigger to let in more light and improve vision

pale or flushed face: blood is sent to the muscles so the skin goes pale, and may flush suddenly when blood rushes to the brain

faster heartbeat and breathing: these speed up so the body has the oxygen and blood it needs to fight or run

trembling: muscles may tremble as they get ready to spring into action

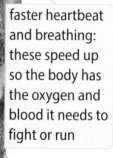

2 How the brain works

Your brain is amazing! It's so complex, scientists still don't fully understand it. Some people say the human brain is the most complex thing in the universe. Your brain has around 100 billion nerve cells, just like there are around 100 billion stars in the Milky Way!

The nerve cells in the brain are called neurons. Neurons send and receive information. They tell our body what to do, and they react to things going on around us. Messages zip between neurons in a matter of milliseconds, all day, every day. Our brain never stops!

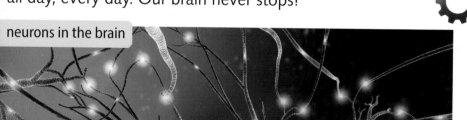

neurons in the brain

a message passing from one neuron to another

Messages cross a gap called a synapse. The messages are made up of chemicals, called neurotransmitters.

synapse

neuron

neurotransmitters

Brain chemistry

Different neurotransmitters pass between neurons to keep the body working. Some neurotransmitters speed things up, like increasing our heart rate when we exercise. Some neurotransmitters slow things down, like slowing our breathing as we get ready to sleep.

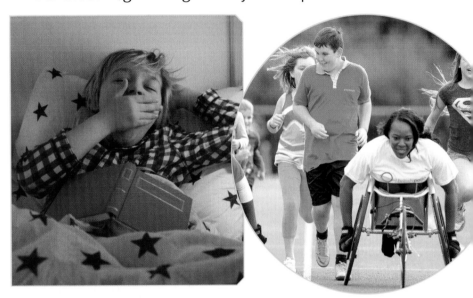

Neurotransmitters can also affect our emotions.

Hormones

Hormones are another type of chemical message.
The **pituitary gland** and the **hypothalamus** in the brain
keep track of all the hormones in the body, and send
messages to other glands in the body to produce more or
fewer hormones. Hormones help our bodies to grow and
develop. They can also affect how we feel.

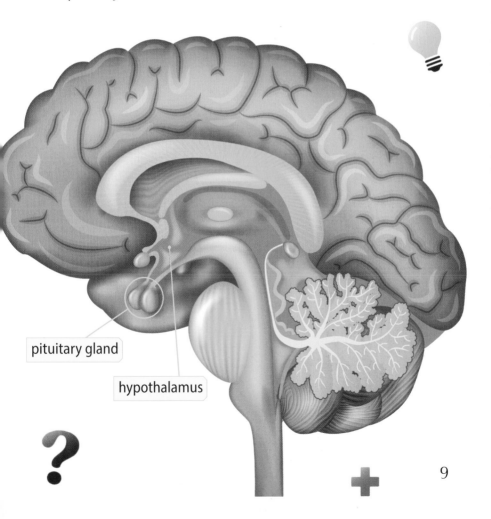

pituitary gland

hypothalamus

9

The nervous system

We have nerves all over our bodies. This is called the nervous system, and it controls everything we do.

When we hear, see, taste, smell or touch something, messages are sent to the brain. The brain then **interprets** the messages and tells us what is going on and what to do.

The brain and the spinal cord make up the central nervous system. The nerves in the other parts of the body are part of the peripheral nervous system. Peripheral means "on the edge".

central nervous system

peripheral nervous system

Sometimes ...

... we have to act quickly and without thinking about it. This is a **reflex** action. Say you touch a spiky plant; nerves in your

fingers send a message to your spinal cord, which sends a message back to your hand to tell it to move, and you quickly snatch your hand away. This all happens without the brain, and in less than one second.

Structure of the brain

The brain has three sections:
the cerebrum (say se-ree-brum),
the cerebellum (say se-reh bell um)
and the brain stem. They all
control different things.

cerebrum
- thinking
- learning
- memory
- emotions
- problem-solving
- language
- taking in information
  from our senses

The three parts of the brain work together to control the things we actively think about, like running, jumping and talking. They also control the things we don't think about, like our organs. It would be quite hard to concentrate on making your heart beat all the time! Luckily, our nervous system takes care of these kinds of things for us.

cerebellum
- movement
- balance
- coordination

brain stem
- breathing
- heart beating
- connects the brain to the spinal cord

The cerebrum is the biggest part of our brain. It's divided into two sides, called hemispheres. The left hemisphere controls the right-hand side of the body. The right hemisphere controls the left-hand side of the body. Both hemispheres communicate with each other.

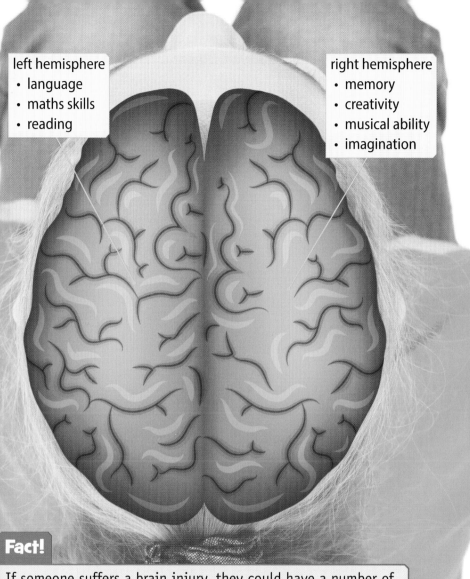

left hemisphere
- language
- maths skills
- reading

right hemisphere
- memory
- creativity
- musical ability
- imagination

Fact!

If someone suffers a brain injury, they could have a number of problems, depending on where the injury happens. For example, if someone hurts the left side of their brain, they might have difficulty moving the right-hand side of their body and have trouble with their speech.

15

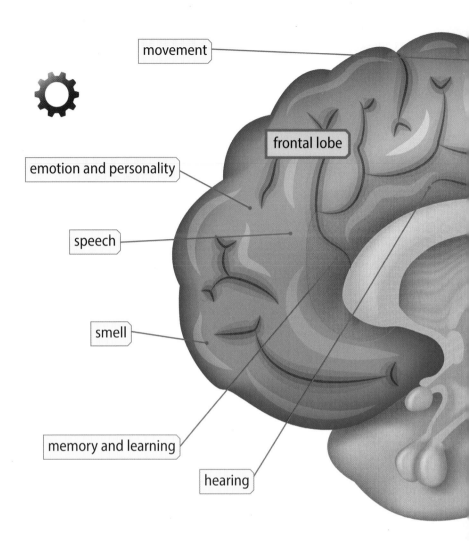

movement

frontal lobe

emotion and personality

speech

smell

memory and learning

hearing

The cerebrum is divided into multiple **lobes**.
Each lobe takes care of different things.

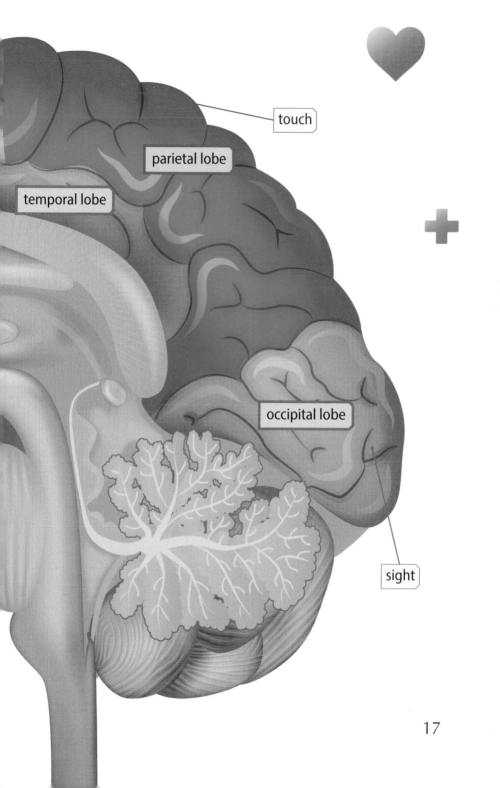

touch

parietal lobe

temporal lobe

occipital lobe

sight

17

Learning new things ?

When you learn something new, your brain has to create a new neural pathway. It's a bit like treading down a pathway of long grass across a field – the more it's pressed down, the easier and quicker it is to travel along the pathway.

Think about when you do something for the first time, like riding a bike. Your brain will have to help you move your legs to pedal, hold onto the handlebars, find your balance, and look where you are going. That's a lot of things to do all at once! But the more you practise, the easier it gets. The brain remembers how to do all of these things at once, and the neural pathways get stronger.

Playing a musical instrument can be great exercise for your brain! Here are all the things a pianist's brain has to think about and control.

Sound: the pianist must listen to what they are doing, and make any changes, such as playing louder/quieter, faster/slower

Sight: they must read two lines of music at once

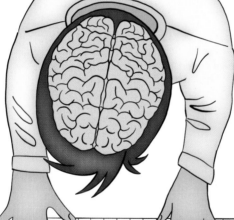

Hands: each hand must play a different line of music at the same time

Fingers: all ten fingers must be controlled to hit the right notes on the keyboard

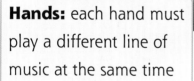

Spatial awareness: pianists learn where each note is on the keyboard and eventually can play without looking at it

3 Our brain and our emotions

The brain controls every part of our body for every single second of our lives. So, it's not surprising to learn that our brain plays a huge part in how we feel.

Emotions are a mix of thoughts, feelings and actions. Our brain remembers past experiences and how we felt. For example, if you were bitten by a dog as a young child, you might be scared of dogs for a long time afterwards. This is because every time you see a dog, your brain remembers that it felt bad to be bitten.

Different things happen to us throughout our lives, and each event will make us feel an emotion. Emotions are complicated, and some feel more intense than others. This circle shows how emotions can be grouped together, yet all feel slightly different.

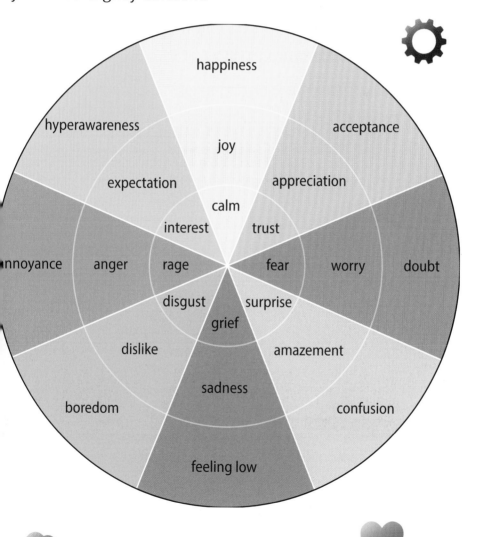

The limbic system

How we feel and how we react to things are controlled by the limbic system.

The limbic system is made up of the thalamus, the hypothalamus, the amygdala and the hippocampus.

The limbic system communicates with the prefrontal cortex, which is part of the cerebrum. The prefrontal cortex is at the very front of our brain and helps us to think carefully and make sensible decisions.

prefrontal cortex

thalamus: sends information to the cerebrum; keeps helpful information and ignores unhelpful information

hypothalamus: releases hormones to keep us at the right temperature and to let us know when we are hungry or thirsty; helps us to express our emotions

amygdala: responds to emotions and links emotions to memories

hippocampus: forms and keeps memories

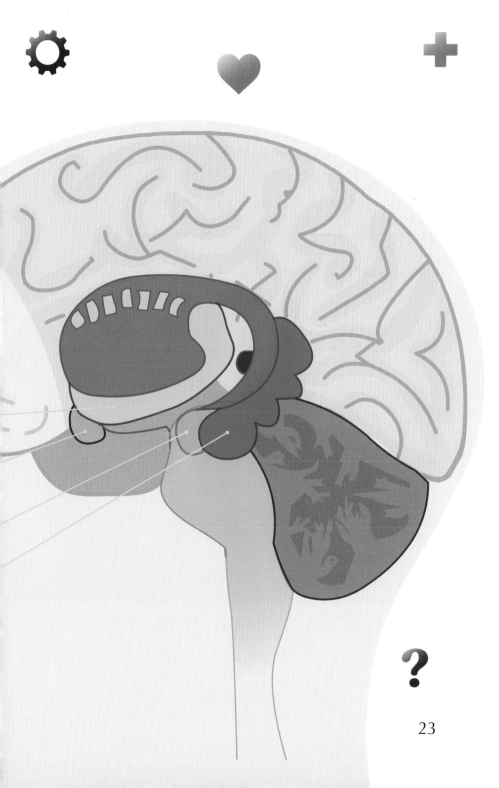

Neurotransmitters

Remember that chemicals passing between neurons in the brain are called neurotransmitters.

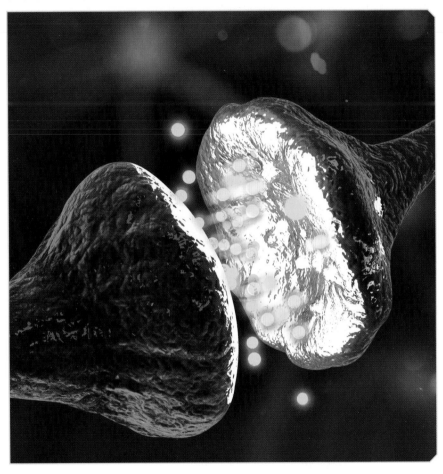

There are lots of different types of neurotransmitters, with different names. They affect the way we feel, and how our body reacts to any situation.

Serotonin

Serotonin is known as the "happy hormone" because it helps us feel calm, relaxed and happy. High levels of serotonin can make us feel really good about ourselves. Some scientists think being indoors too much can lead to low levels of serotonin. To get more, simply go outside! Even if it's cloudy, your brain will benefit from being exposed to sunlight.

Facts!

- Our intestines have neurons too.
- Most of our serotonin is made in the intestines.
- Neurons in our brain and intestines send messages to each other.
- Eating healthily can help increase our serotonin levels.

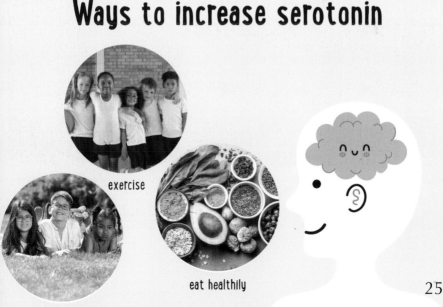

Ways to increase serotonin

exercise

eat healthily

spend time outside

Dopamine

Dopamine is another feel-good neurotransmitter. Your brain releases dopamine as a reward if you achieve a goal. Your goal could be anything from climbing Mount Everest to reaching the next level on a computer game! Dopamine can motivate you to achieve your goals. Lower levels of dopamine can make it harder to get motivated.

Ways to increase dopamine

exercise

eat protein

get plenty of sleep

The downside to dopamine is that it can make you want more! So, you might take more risks and become overly competitive.

Fact!

Getting likes or comments on social media can make the brain produce dopamine. This is why it's easy to get addicted to social media, and why it can make people feel bad. If they don't get any likes or comments, they don't get the "dopamine hit".

Adrenaline

Remember the fight or flight response? When your brain thinks a situation is dangerous, it tells the **adrenal glands** to produce adrenaline. This happens incredibly quickly, and is known as an "adrenaline rush". It makes your heart beat faster and prepares the muscles to react quickly.

Some people like to do things like ride rollercoasters or extreme sports to get an adrenaline rush. Releasing adrenaline in positive ways can help raise serotonin levels, making you feel good.

However, if your body often makes adrenaline because of stress and anxiety, it can make you feel bad. It can give you headaches and make you feel anxious.

Ways to decrease adrenaline

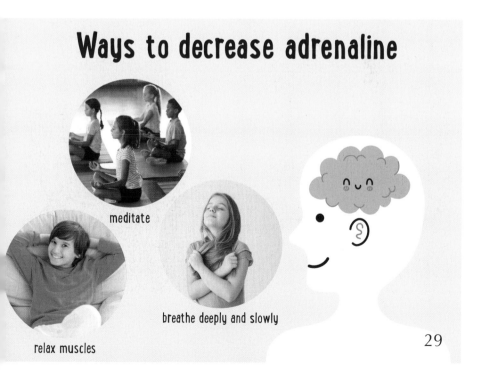

meditate

breathe deeply and slowly

relax muscles

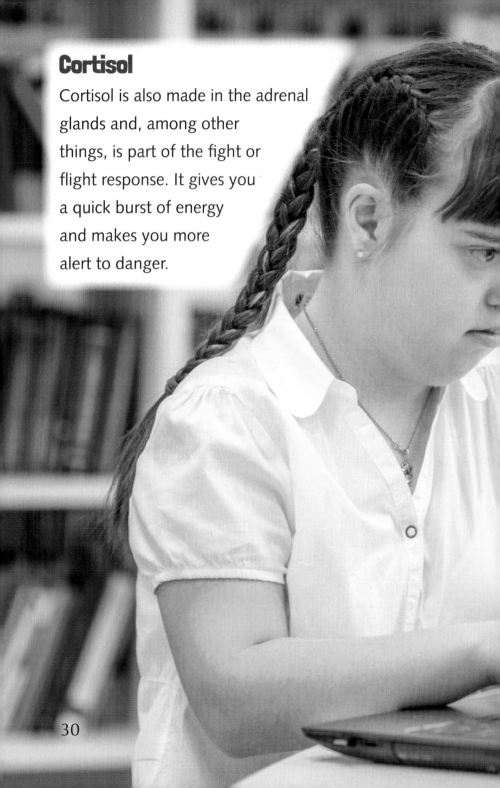

Cortisol

Cortisol is also made in the adrenal glands and, among other things, is part of the fight or flight response. It gives you a quick burst of energy and makes you more alert to danger.

The fight or flight response was helpful for early humans, and it can also be helpful for us in some situations. But things like exams, or difficulties at home or at school can make us feel stressed, so the brain thinks we're in danger. Then cortisol is released when we don't really need it. This can give us headaches, make us feel anxious and even a little bit sick.

Ways to decrease cortisol

meditate

breathe deeply and slowly

talk to someone

Endorphins

Endorphins make us feel pleasure and reduce pain. If you hurt yourself, endorphins are quickly released to help dull the pain.

When we do fun activities, endorphins flow through our body and make us feel great.

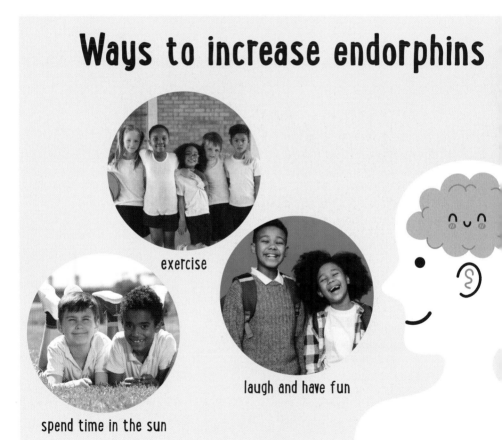

Ways to increase endorphins

exercise

laugh and have fun

spend time in the sun

4 Growing body, growing brain

The brain is one of the first organs to develop when we are still inside the womb. It starts to develop when a baby is the size of a blueberry!

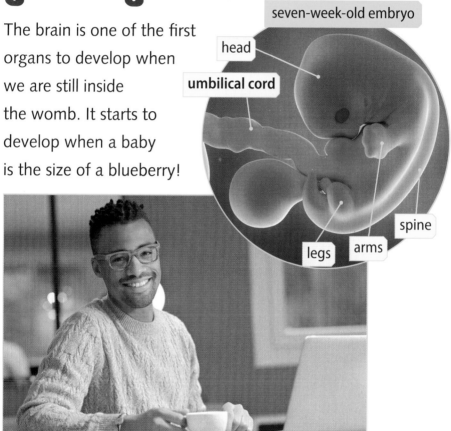

seven-week-old embryo

head

umbilical cord

spine

legs

arms

The brain is also the last organ to finish growing. You'll be around 25 years old by the time your brain is fully developed.

Adolescence is the time between childhood and adulthood. Lots of changes happen in your brain during adolescence as the different parts gradually become connected.

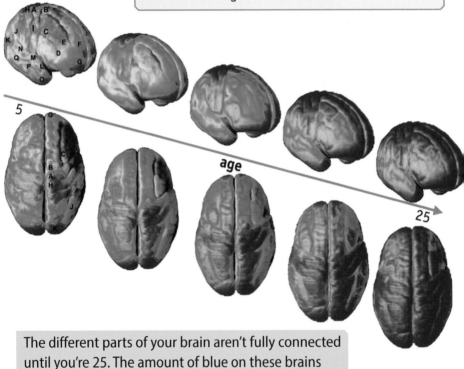

The different parts of your brain aren't fully connected until you're 25. The amount of blue on these brains show how many connections there are.

The prefrontal cortex is the last part of your brain to finish developing.

The prefrontal cortex helps you to think clearly and **regulate** your emotions. But because it's the last part of your brain to finish developing, children and teenagers can find it hard to regulate their emotions. It can be easy to become over-excited or very sad about something really quickly. Teenage brains react more strongly to dopamine, and have more of it. This makes them take more risks than adults.

How your brain develops depends on different things. Everybody's brain develops differently because we are all unique and have different life experiences.

Brain development can be affected by:

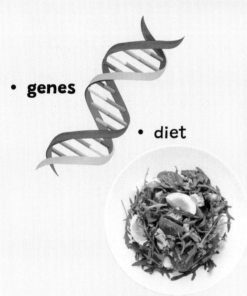

- **genes**

- **diet**

- environment (where you live)

- **sleep patterns**

- **physical experiences**

- **emotional experiences**

Neuroplasticity

Just as it takes a while to learn a new skill, it takes a while to learn how to deal with different situations.

Children and teenagers can find it hard to make decisions in difficult situations because their brain doesn't have enough experiences or memories to call on yet. Just like when you learn a new skill and form a new neural pathway, your brain needs to form neural pathways for **critical thought** and **logical thought**. It takes time to learn how to make sensible, rational decisions.

Neuroplasticity

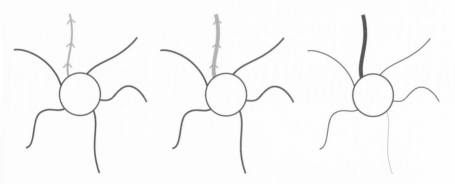

Neurons fire in new directions when we learn something new.

The more we repeat the action, the stronger the pathway becomes.

Any pathways that stop being used get weaker and weaker.

Emotional regulation

Anyone – child, teenager or adult – going through
a difficult time may find it hard to regulate their emotions.
They could get angry easily or feel **depressed**. This can
happen if we are more easily stressed because of school or
work, friendship or family problems, or upsetting events.
If you find yourself in a difficult situation, your emotions
might feel overwhelming.

All emotions are important. We might think of some
as "bad" and others as "good" but they all help us.
For example, feeling angry that you failed
a test could make you study harder
next time. Or doing a particular
activity might make you feel
happy, so you know to keep
taking part. And showing
our emotions to others
can help them
to understand
you better.

Life is full of ups and downs, a bit like a rollercoaster. It's normal to feel things like sadness, jealousy or anxiety. Our brain needs us to express the right emotion for each situation.

If you suppress certain emotions and pretend to be happy, this won't stop your brain producing too much adrenaline and cortisol. This can cause physical and emotional problems, like not being able to sleep or relax properly.

Coping with emotions

The next time you experience something difficult, try to stop and think for a moment. Count to ten and ask yourself:

✓ How am I feeling?

✓ Which emotion is it?

✓ What has made me feel this way?

Sometimes, just paying attention to and understanding how we feel is enough to help us calm down. We need to give our prefrontal cortex a chance to catch up with our limbic system.

Your brain needs lots of oxygen to work properly, so if you take some deep breaths, you might find that you feel calmer.

You can also try to use neuroplasticity to help you. If you gradually tell yourself more positive messages, over time you can feel better.

For example, you might often tell yourself that you're not very clever and you'll never do well at school. Your neural pathway for this thought will be very strong because you think it all the time and you believe it's the truth.

Ideas to help

talking to a friend

deep breathing

writing a journal

getting outside

doing some exercise

If you gradually tell yourself a new, positive message, you can start believing that instead.

I'm doing better because I kept trying. I have good perseverance.

Glossary

adrenal glands small organs that make hormones

critical thought thinking very carefully

depressed feeling constantly sad

evolved developed gradually

genes small sections of DNA that determine lots of different things about us, like how we look

hypothalamus area of the brain controlling body temperature and heart rate

interprets understands the meaning of something

lobes parts that are rounded and stick out from the main part

logical thought using evidence to think in an ordered way

pituitary gland a small organ at the base of the brain that makes hormones

reflex an involuntary, quick reaction

regulate control, manage

umbilical cord cord that links an unborn baby to its mother inside the womb

Index

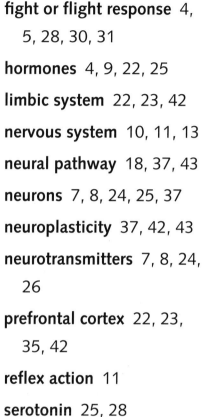

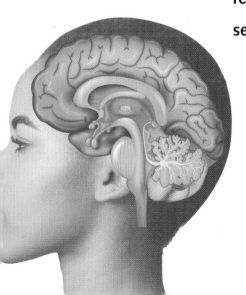

Boosting neurotransmitters

serotonin

adrenaline

endorphins

cortisol

?

dopamine

47

:: Ideas for reading ::

Written by Christine Whitney
Primary Literacy Consultant

Reading objectives:
- identify and discuss themes in a wide range of writing
- retrieve, record and present information from non-fiction
- explain the meaning of words in context
- identify main ideas drawn from more than one paragraph and summarise these

Spoken language objectives:
- participate in discussion
- speculate, hypothesise, imagine and explore ideas through talk
- ask relevant questions

Curriculum links: Science: Animals, including humans: recognise the impact of diet, exercise, drugs and lifestyle on the way bodies function

Interest words: emotions, neurons, adrenaline

Build a context for reading

- Read the title of the book and play *Five in three*! Ask children to share five facts they know about the brain to each other in three minutes.
- Ask children to explain the meaning of *Meet Your Brain*. What do they predict the content of the book to be?
- Ask children to compose a question about the brain that they hope to find the answer to in the book.

Understand and apply reading strategies

- Read Chapter 1 together. Ask children to summarise what they have learnt about the evolution of the brain.
- Continue to read together up to the end of Chapter 2. Give these titles to the children in the group - *Brain chemistry, Hormones, The nervous system, Structure of the brain, Learning new things*. Ask them to explain the part played by their section in the working of the brain.
- Read together Chapter 3. Ask children to complete this sentence *The downside to dopamine is ...*
- Read on to the end of p37. How is *neuroplasticity* related to the growing brain?